Once Familiar

poems by

Barbara Ford

Finishing Line Press
Georgetown, Kentucky

Once Familiar

Copyright © 2016 by Barbara Ford
ISBN 978-1-944899-18-9 First Edition
All rights reserved under International and Pan-American Copyright Conventions. No part of this book may be reproduced in any manner whatsoever without written permission from the publisher, except in the case of brief quotations embodied in critical articles and reviews.

ACKNOWLEDGMENTS

Many thanks to the following journals and anthologies in which these poems, sometimes in earlier versions, first appeared:

Hair Pieces: Sonoma County Writing Practice Anthology: "Open Your Window"
Pilgrimage; reprinted in the anthology *Telling It Real*: "Standing Invitation"
Transnational Literature: "Age"
Footnotes: Sonoma County Writing Practice Anthology: "The News from Santa Fe," originally titled "We Always Signed Always"
Democracy of Poets, Aspen Poets' Society Anthology: "Exploration"
Plainsongs: "What Remains Must Be Mended"
Common Ground Review; reprinted in the anthology *Parade of Poets*: "Found. Lost."

Editor: Christen Kincaid

Cover Art: Suzie Ryan

Author Photo: Kit Hedman, www.kithedmanfineartphotography.com

Cover Design: Elizabeth Maines

Printed in the USA on acid-free paper.
Order online: www.finishinglinepress.com
         also available on amazon.com

Author inquiries and mail orders:
Finishing Line Press
P. O. Box 1626
Georgetown, Kentucky 40324
U. S. A.

Table of Contents

Open Your Window 1
Standing Invitation 2
Out of the West 3
Reading Borges 5
Revelations 6
Blood Sister 7
Angle of Suppose 9
Archives 10
Visiting You in the Desert 12
Age. 13
Kneeling at the Gates 14
Rothko 15
Thanksgiving 16
Childhood 17
The News from Santa Fe 18
Exploration 20
Equinox 21
Genealogy 22
You Know Who You Are 23
The Argument 24
What Remains Must Be Mended 25
Found. Lost. 26
The Refrain 27
La Giaconda 28
Bespoken 29
Aloft 30

For CoCo

*Emptiness is the mother of all things
—from a fortune cookie*

Open Your Window

A poem blows across the floor.
It's the one I've wanted to send you.

Expect a breeze
tomorrow morning.

The future's been lifted
out of my slow hands.

Standing Invitation

Tell me your rich and terrible story.
The scarlet flush of anger?
Don't leave it out.
Include each irreversible wave of loss.
Trust me as witness, again.

We've learned how to weather the other,
how to zip our sleeping bags together
and make room for interlacing dreams,
dirges, and the whisper of what remains.

When we're filled up,
weighty and complete,
we'll unzip.
You'll fly to your coastal lake,
and I to the spine of mountains
I cannot live away from.

If we once asked something else
of friendship it's a ghost long gone.
Bring me who you are now.
Recently my heart has grown
wide enough to bear it.

Out of the West

A bridge span and light years
away from The City
was my town—clear-aired,
tree-lined, a *masala* of coastal folk,
nuclear families, students
from the twelve corners of the earth
constellated around the University
as matrix and heartbeat;
bay at its western feet,
eastern hills as backdrop
to children walking to school
who knew how to say 'campanile'
and 'eucalyptus' before kindergarten;
place of first lost tooth,
chicken pox, my hand
on a corduroy shoulder
learning how to waltz,
the evening fog
constant as a mother,
greening the gardens
with its invisible water.
When I was taken away
my town taught me homesickness,
and later, when I came back,
unrequited love, and how
they can ache in the same way.
When I left for good
I found out home
is a tattoo that can't be erased,
even if those who stay
steal it and make it theirs—
immigrant philosophers,
prophets and panhandlers,

the radically chic and first-
on-the-block hippies turned
shopkeepers and householders.
Requisitioned and reshaped
by the outspoken, the outraged,
and the politically outrageous—
my first place,
my original sin,
my maiden name,
Berkeley.

Reading Borges

We imagine a tiger
as though one were
sprawled at our feet,
striped and purring.

The hands of the clock
move imperceptibly
to elude the notice
of that terrifying eye.

The minute the phone rings
everything is instantly
pulled out of one place
and pushed into another,

wild things hustled back
into the cage of our thoughts
to resume the pace,
scavenging for food.

Except when the leap
out the window is successful,
the receiver knocked off its cradle
by a demure roar.

Revelations

When asked how goes my spiritual practice
I enter the room with no door,

write my answer on a sheet of paper,
strike a match to incinerate the words

for transport in an envelope,
requesting the reader

to unseal it in moonlight,
with instructions to the wind

to lift the smoke and ashes
into its fierce arms,

revealing all there is to say,
in the language one must use

when speaking
of such matters.

Blood Sister

Although not the bright maroon
of plastic-wrapped organs
at the butcher's, they felt like fresh
liver relieved of half its density

as each warm clot slithered blackly
through my fingers, awash in the blood
streaming from my friend's uterus.
The child was not going to be born,

not then, not there. It was five years
before he held fast to the helm,
more than once frightening us
with those dark clotted clumps

at the three month mark.
In messy triumph he sailed into port
at full term, tumbling from the womb
onto his parents' queen-sized bed

while a handful of friends gripped
coffee mugs in the living room.
That his mother and I no longer speak
is a faded armchair I sit in everyday.

Did the boy notice when we stopped
championing each other, how we
gradually rendered our friendship
into a bleating goat tethered to a stake?

Wasn't he our principal witness
as we took turns shredding the warm
animal of kinship into an unrecognizable
thing? And after, how we let its last blood

reach deep, down into the same dirt
where we'd buried the fragrant placenta
eighteen winters earlier, both of us laughing
at our awkwardness with the shovel.

Angle of Suppose

1. Divestiture

How to fill
the hollow holidays

emptied of stuffing
and rags of shoulds

try feathers
try wind

try knowing how rare
true emptiness is.

2. Destiny

Flying through the mist
we open the map one fold at a time

trusting we will see the mountain's outline
well before the breath of the propeller

lifts the petals of edelweiss
embedded in the granite face of eternity.

Archives

It's in black and white, this photo,
with an unmemorable composition
in a narrow range of grays.
If you squint, my father and I
will disappear right off the beach
like a magic act on that Santa Cruz
morning dull with overcast,
the kind of pale day you know
will end in a wicked scald of a sunburn
if you're too careless or carefree.
White ruffles of foam surround Dad's
and my feet at the edge of the Pacific,
we've just been told to hold still
by my mother who's about to click.
Both my eyebrows are slightly raised
in expectancy, one arm crooked upwards
for my hand to reach his, small head
level with the waistband of his trunks.
He was not a recreational man,
his dislike of swimming a family fact,
but there he is, toes sunk in wet sand,
in the only shot of the two of us alone
out of the disheveled stack snapped
in the years he was alive.
We're side by side, hand in hand,
not a sibling in sight,
just the distant pier thrusting
hard angles into the water.
You can't tell if he's smiling,
or which way his head is turned,

because the photograph chops
him off just above where his heart
was beating. I like to think
he looked happy.

Visiting You in the Desert

As you lie there,
covered in dust and dried
seed pods, I bring you water,

that you might stop
drinking tears
to lessen your thirst.

To know you have loved,
and loved through it all,
is much.

To be certain you gave
everything off your shelves,
even after the larder was reduced

to the crumbs and rinds of habit,
every drop of crimson juice gone
from years of steady extraction.

Next time, set a place
for your heart at the table.
Help yourself to a full plate.

Age

Useful as insulation against the coldness of youth
is the frittata of years studded with the momentous

and the miniscule, the almost but not-quite-
forgotten gem. To have seen the queen

without meaning to, to recall the indelible
green of the hat and dress she wore

as she waved to the crowd with its parade
of noses pressed up to the palace gates.

The thrill of dialing one's mother in California
from a Bayswater hotel room long before cell phones

to announce her daughter had happened
upon a royal sighting,

the answering glee that trilled transatlantically
as she sank into a chair,

talking to London *for God's sake*,
holding half a pearl in her hand

while across the ocean of her mind's eye
the other half glowed in mine.

Kneeling at the Gates

at the bakery
asking again
for salmon

at the tavern
asking again
for rebirth

at the prison
asking again
for a belly laugh

at the altar
asking again
for a guarantee

at the cradle
asking again
for a map

at the ocean
asking again
for altitude

at graveside
asking again
for love

on our knees
asking again
asking, again

Rothko

Swallowed by what you uncovered,
with your giants before them

no one shall declare
that nothing is new.

You said no words are required,
silence is so accurate.

In those hours
before you were discovered

in a field of viscous red,
did you pass through unnameable colors,

or must that, too,
remain unsayable?

Thanksgiving

The transparent residue
of her weeklong stay
has settled in various rooms,
most visible when struck
by afternoon light,
like the sudden sighting
of a cobweb, or a shed skin.
No scent loiters,
although the air itself
bears a faint imprint
of her brief existence here.

For days after she departed
the house was a mansion,
every moment a golden coin,
my lover the perfect man.
This she accomplished
merely by coming, then going,
as if she'd been the parent
and I the child put in jail overnight
to learn how profound it is
to be free.

In gratitude I unwrap
the great gift of her leaving,
the limp relief of waving adieu
to a retinue of expectations
about the exchange rates
applied to vacations.

Childhood

They gave us a game board
with painted squares
and stacks of colored chips.

We played, although
when we got tired
our attention waned.

They removed pieces,
switched the colors
while we were napping.

In our youthful resilience
we adjusted
to each new version.

By the time we were grown
there was one square left,
piled with every chip in the house.

We went upstairs
to pack our bags for the world.
Our graduation present

was the rule book,
perfect for second guessers,
missing half its pages.

The News from Santa Fe

I didn't mind
that you never sent me
a birthday card
after I heard how
unwell you'd felt,
but I went everyday
to the post office
until I found out
what happened.
Your postcard
from the Cuban café
showed up instead,
a few tasty words
about an evening
the week before.
That was it.
The last piece of mail
I ever got from you,
rotund handwriting
I could pick out
of a lineup, just
one more thing
I loved about you.
I've been wondering
about our twenty
years of letters.
Shall your daughter
have that part
of you, or is fire
best? Let me know,

remind me what
to keep and what
to let go. If there's
an etiquette to death
you've had time
to learn the ropes.
Send me a birthday dream.
You know I don't care
if it's late.

Exploration

Once, he planted his private flag
on the slope of her breast,
where he claimed ownership
of the mole he discovered there,
a miniature brown hillock
on which he built a tiny hut
to use for rest and refuge
during his wanderings
over the pale landscape of her skin.
Later, they lost each other,
as young lovers will,
called by other voices, places.
Occasionally, what's left
of his small shelter appears
in the morning mirror—
vast sweep of sky
showing through the thatch,
birds' nests balanced on rafters,
flag shredded by the storms
that visit every woman's breast
as she climbs and descends,
climbs and descends.

Equinox

The insistent forsythia
raises her yellow arms

while we watch for ice
on the sidewalk.

The blackbird, red-winged,
flutes his intent

as ants begin their drone
underground.

Each corner of the world
is dusted daily by the wind

toppling brooms
laden with winter's leavings.

With half-closed eyes
life drinks the holy horizon

forging the key for unlocking
its paint box.

When the clock of heaven
chimes the quarter hour

we lurch from hibernation
ravenous as a bear.

Genealogy

Nesting in my family tree
are solitude and loneliness

on branches so close
the birds often sit on one

while looking for insects
on the other.

You Know Who You Are

It's always you who calls me
when I'm having a bad day,
that's the kind of radar you have.
After I blurt my confession,
I hear you nodding, confident
you know exactly what I mean
because of what your bad days
are like, those hurtling comets
manned by mammoth hornets in heat,
best combated wearing a helmet
while swinging grappling hooks
and lassoes nicked from the Valkyries.
Mine arrive from another sector,
an inner Mongolia with set designs
stolen from Dust Bowl internment camps.
You have never been there.
How I covet your glasses,
the ones that spy the possibilities
crouching in every corner,
or the sparkly pair that reliably
eyeballs the end in sight.
Sometimes I practice using
your words: *priorities, productivity,*
and the one that fits your firm hands
like a glove, *communication.*
On my truly horrid days,
only your voice can play the usher.
You hand me a program,
then flashlight me to a row
in the theatre where a seat's
been saved right up close to yours.
All I need now is a triple feature.

The Argument
   for Joe

One deer among the markers,
countless others hidden in the pines.

The wind and resident birds
oddly absent today.

In the stillness graveyards are known for,
you harangue me with your raucous
magpie of a voice,

telling me what you'd give
for all the time I squander
mourning you.

What Remains Must Be Mended

The Chinese jacket has been scissored to pieces
Shorn of shape, stripped of original purpose
My long ago sister, I share the fruit of your labor
Out and around, sectioned like an orange

Infinitely-petaled peonies and chrysanthemums
Dragons draped in shimmering scales
Opulent butterflies with tails quivering above the earth
The stream of riches issuing from your small hands

Today, my thin sharp needle threads its way
Through the field of your invisible stitches
Making a new trail of red on the crumbling silk
While I watch you across the silence of distance

Back crooked, eyes fading, bent fingers
flying over the empress's morning coat
Up to the day you were cast from court
With a beggar's purse and a tapping stick

Sister of another century, after your time
It was decreed forbidden, but later, later
Though the slick thread escapes the needle
These faraway hands trace your fate

As I prick my thumb again and again
My intractable heart stitches its demand
For your return with new eyes
To live a hundred fruitful lives

In exchange for the beauty
That blinded my forsaken sister.

Found. Lost.

As known, the weight was a comfort,
each layer applied evenly,

smoothed with a mental spatula,
a near perfect fit, familiar.

Wildly proud of my rich clothing,
coat of family, cloak of kin,

I showed off my resplendent self,
flashing pictures, eager to say

here's the hard proof of belonging,
faces, places, names, what we ate.

Later, as happens, it ended.
First, the scorch of volcanic grief

then chills, only one garment left me:
this holy threadbare longing.

The Refrain

Five of us lie on our bellies in the Santa Monica sand
and agree to say our mantras out loud.

A few cigarettes are lighted against the breeze.

First Jen says hers, then Josie, then the guys.

No one mentions how we've carried them inside for years,
layered in muteness, only that they sound alike, more or less.

It's my turn, I'm last, but the tight fist of my heart
won't open to release its consecrated wafer,
flesh of my flesh.

Tied by the matched hands of faith and fear,
I can't budge the Sanskrit knot of my tongue,

as if it's been planted in the mouth of a vessel
unwilling to be emptied of its one chance
at transcendence.

La Giaconda

When the painter
must prepare
the impossible violet
for depicting snow
at twilight,
close the door
to the studio.
Step lightly
on the stairs,
quiet the beets
in their bubbling red sea.
We cannot know
all things and this
is what saves us.
We cannot remember
all that was once familiar.
Were he to return,
would Leonardo
create her smile
a second time?

Bespoken

There have been times
in a black forest
when a moment arrives
on tiny wings of flame,
a moment that allows me
to see how it fits,
the shape of what connects us
each to each.

I don't want you to know
how many years and closets
I have searched for that sign,
that proof.
Like this morning,
your note,
the yellow post-it.

It wasn't the *love you*,
it was the two words
that followed
like a small train,
so much.
I saw how it all fits,
just then,
just for a moment.

Aloft

I went away from poetry
for the weekend.
It was a happy miss
to spend two days
in wordlessness,

not counting the poem
that fell in my lap
on Saturday morning,
or the short one
I asked him to read

that said what I
didn't know how to say
even though I'd written it
just the other day.
Throughout those

forty-eight hours
words were really farthest
from my thoughts,
but I caught myself
in restlessness,

looking longingly
at the chair—
the one I climb into
to fly to the country
I love best.

West Coast native Barbara Ford started out as a visual artist, studying drawing, painting and printmaking at the California College of Arts and Crafts, followed by years of boomeranging around the country. Her smörgasbord of jobs includes work in bike shops, a talent agency, umpteen restaurants, an art factory, several printmaking studios, and a ministorage facility. Habitual scrawling in notebooks and writing fat letters to the living and the dead ultimately landed her hard in the arms of poetry. She moved to central Colorado in 2005 to join the poets who live with their heads in the clouds. Her hour-long radio show, *Poets and Minstrels*, is in its tenth year at KHEN in Salida. Her poems have been published in journals and anthologies, including *Spillway, Pilgrimage, So It Goes* and others. She has presented her poetry at festivals and conferences all over the state.

www.ingramcontent.com/pod-product-compliance
Lightning Source LLC
Chambersburg PA
CBHW060225050426
42446CB00013B/3176